Published by Familius LLC, www.familius.com
1254 Commerce Way, Sanger, CA 93657

Familius books are available at special discounts for bulk purchases, whether for
sales promotions or for family or corporate use. For more information, contact
Familius Sales at 559-876-2170 or email orders@familius.com.

Library of Congress Control Number: 2020939144

Print ISBN 9781641701983
Ebook ISBN 9781641703772
KF 9781641704014
FE 9781641704250

Printed in the China
Edited by Peg Sandkam and Lacey Wulf
Cover and book design by Brooke Jorden

10 9 8 7 6 5 4 3 2 1

First Edition

# CONTENTS

LARA LYN CARTER

# SKINNY SOUTHERN BAKING

**65** GLUTEN-FREE, DAIRY-FREE, REFINED SUGAR-FREE SOUTHERN CLASSICS

FAMILIUS

Dedicated to my "Mimi," Mittie Hayes Chitty.

So much more than my maternal grandmother, she was my hero. She was loving, strong, beautiful, tough as nails, a follower of Christ, and she was "Mimi." She loved family, cooking, fishing, playing Bridge, board games, reading, and working in her yard. If you knew her, chances are you had one of the millions of pound cakes she made, or her cheese wafers or Lane cakes.

I spent weeks with her every summer well into my teenage years when most teenagers would rather be hanging out with friends. Well, to me, she was my friend as well as my grandmother. The summer I turned sixteen, the first place I wanted to drive was to see her two hours away. I drove her everywhere that summer in my car!

She taught me a lot about cooking. In fact, all of our family gatherings revolved around food. She was a natural in the kitchen, she just knew how to make delicious food and make people feel like you meant the world to her through her cooking.

I have been called "little Mittie" by several in my family, and what an amazing compliment that is to me! I was blessed to have had her with me for almost thirty-six years and there is still not a day that goes by I wouldn't give anything to pick up that phone and hear her voice or sit with her and eat a slice of one of her pound cakes. I hope at the end of the day she looks down on me from heaven with a big smile and I have made her proud.

Love you, Mimi!

# CONTENTS

FOREWORD BY MARC SUMMERS | VII

## COOKIES | 1

Almond Cookies | 2

Coconut Shortbread Cookies | 5

Ginger Cookies | 6

Dylan's Hot Chocolate Cookies | 9

Pumpkin Spice Cookies | 10

Oatmeal Raisin Cookies | 13

Thumbprint Cookies | 14

Oatmeal, Apricot, and Pistachio Cookies | 17

Peanut Butter Cookies | 18

Butter Pecan Cookies | 21

Coconut Cream Cheese Snowballs | 22

## COBBLERS, BARS, AND BROWNIES | 25

Blueberry Cobbler | 26

Chocolate Cobbler | 28

Apple Cream Cheese Cobbler | 29

Mrs. Joy's Congo Bars | 31

Blondies | 32

Pecan Pie Gooey Bars | 34

PB&J Bars | 35

Toffee Bars | 36

Pumpkin Pecan Oatmeal Bars | 38

Double Chocolate Brownies | 39

### CAKES | 41

Orange Chiffon Cake | 42

Apple Spice Cake | 45

Peanut Butter Banana Coffeecake | 46

German Chocolate Cake | 49

Honey Cake | 50

Carrot Cupcakes | 53

Cola Cake | 54

Lemon Coconut Cupcakes | 57

Fig Upside-Down Cake | 58

Pumpkin Gingersnap Cheesecake | 59

### MUFFINS AND BREADS | 61

Lemon Poppy Seed and Lavender Bread | 62

Apple, Cheddar, and Rosemary Biscuits | 63

Pumpkin Cranberry Nut Bread | 65

Gingerbread | 66

Morning Glory Muffins | 69

Oatmeal Blueberry Almond Muffins | 70

Banana Chocolate Chip Muffins | 73

Cinnamon Pecan Muffins | 74

Peach Cobbler Muffins | 75

Banana Nut Bread | 77

### PIES | 79

Almond Flour Pie Crust | 80

Chocolate Pie Crust | 82

Coconut Flour Pie Crust | 83

Death by Chocolate Pie Filling | 85

Beau's Peanut Butter Pie Filling | 86

Crustless Coconut Pie | 87

Lemon Blueberry Pie | 89

Georgia Pecan-Crusted Pumpkin Pie | 90

### THE SAVORY SIDE OF THINGS | 93

Parmesan Cheese Straws | 94

Savory Olive and Rosemary Bread Pudding | 97

Chicken and Portobello Mushroom Pot Pie | 98

Pumpkin Cornbread | 101

Mama's Thanksgiving Dressing | 102

Spinach and Feta Muffins | 103

Mimi's Cheese Straws | 104

Garlic and Herb Flatbread | 107

Herb Biscuits | 108

Almond Flour Biscuits | 111

### THIS AND THAT | 113

Fig Butter | 114

Fruit Preserves | 117

Christopher's Pepper Jelly | 118

Whipped Cream | 119

Powdered Coconut Sugar | 119

Lemon Curd | 120

Chocolate Sauce | 123

# FOREWORD

I recognized Lara Lyn's talents both on camera and in her cooking. You cannot teach what comes naturally to Lara Lyn. And once that Southern charm takes over, you feel as if you have known her forever.

Researching not only for her and her family's health but also for the many other people that live a gluten-free, refined sugar–free, and dairy-free life, Lara Lyn has taken her passion for cooking and a clean-eating lifestyle in a direction like no other.

Unwilling to compromise on flavor, she has worked diligently to ensure her recipes are delicious. She knows how much this type of book is needed to keep everyone's menus varied. She has seen and heard from people who view her on television, and they are elated to have delicious recipes that fit their lifestyle.

Lara Lyn is on the cusp of a lifestyle that is going to continue to grow as people learn more and want to take control of their health. And she is doing it deliciously!

—*Marc Summers*

Marc Summers is Executive Producer and co-host of *Double Dare* on Nickelodeon. He is best known as the host of *Unwrapped*, one of the longest-running series on the Food Network. Marc was the original host of *Food Network Star* and has been a guest on *The Tonight Show, Oprah,* and *The Howard Stern Show.*

# CHAPTER 1

## COOKIES

# ALMOND COOKIES

*My mama's favorite flavor: almond. Not too sweet but with all of that almond flavor, these cookies are perfect for any occasion.*

1/4 CUP COCONUT OIL

1 CUP COCONUT SUGAR

2 TEASPOONS ALMOND EXTRACT

2 EGGS AT ROOM TEMPERATURE

2 CUPS ALMOND FLOUR

1/2 TEASPOON BAKING SODA

1/2 TEASPOON FINE SEA SALT

1 CUP SLIVERED ALMONDS

1   Preheat the oven to 350 degrees and line a baking sheet with parchment paper.

2   In a large bowl, combine the coconut oil, coconut sugar, almond extract, and eggs.

3   Add the dry ingredients to the wet ingredients and mix well. Stir in the almonds last.

4   Use a melon ball scoop to put the dough on the baking sheet. The cookies will spread, so leave a couple of inches between each cookie.

5   Bake for 14 minutes.

# COCONUT SHORTBREAD COOKIES

*Dylan loves to use cookie cutters to make different shapes. This recipe is perfect for some mommy-and-me time in the kitchen.*

1 2/3 CUPS COCONUT FLOUR
1/2 CUP COCONUT OIL
4 OUNCES MAPLE SYRUP

1 TABLESPOON PLANT-BASED BUTTER, MELTED
1 TEASPOON PURE VANILLA

1. Preheat the oven to 350 degrees and line a baking sheet with parchment paper.

2. In a mixing bowl, combine all ingredients until smooth. Then let the mixture sit for 7 minutes to allow the coconut flour to absorb the liquid.

3. Roll the dough into a ball and place on a piece of parchment paper. Place another piece of parchment paper on top and roll the dough into about 1/4-inch thickness.

4. Using the cookie cutter of your choice, cut the cookies out. Carefully arrange the cookies on the baking sheet. Continue rerolling the remaining dough until all is used.

5. Bake the cookies for 10–12 minutes.

6. Cool completely before decorating.

HELPFUL TIP! To make cutting easier, dip the cookie cutter into warm water before each cut.
DECORATING IDEA! I love to dip part of the cookie in melted chocolate or even add some unsweetened coconut.

# GINGER COOKIES

*These ginger cookies are soft, delicious, and full of the spices we think of at Christmas. They also freeze great, so make an extra batch and save them for a rainy day.*

2 1/4 CUPS ALMOND FLOUR, TIGHTLY PACKED

1/2 CUP COCONUT SUGAR

1/2 TEASPOON BAKING POWDER

1/4 TEASPOON BAKING SODA

1 TEASPOON CINNAMON

1 TEASPOON NUTMEG

1 TEASPOON CLOVE

2 TEASPOONS GINGER

3 EGGS

1/4 CUP MOLASSES

1/4 CUP COCONUT OIL

1   Preheat the oven to 350 degrees and line a baking sheet with parchment paper.

2   Combine the dry ingredients and break up any clumps in the flour or sugar with a fork.

3   In a separate bowl, mix the wet ingredients.

4   Slowly stir the wet ingredients into the dry ingredients and mix well.

5   Shape the cookies into circles and arrange them on the baking sheet.

6   Bake for 12–15 minutes.

7   Cool completely and enjoy!

# DYLAN'S HOT CHOCOLATE COOKIES

*If Santa could pick only one cookie to have on Christmas Eve, this would be the one he would choose! Dylan agrees!*

◇◇◇◇◇◇◇◇◇◇◇◇◇◇◇◇◇◇◇◇◇◇◇◇◇◇◇◇◇◇◇◇◇◇◇◇◇◇◇◇◇◇◇◇◇◇◇◇

4 TABLESPOONS ORGANIC BUTTER AT ROOM TEMPERATURE

1/4 CUP COCONUT OIL

3/4 CUP COCONUT SUGAR

2 TABLESPOONS D'VASH DATE NECTAR

2 TEASPOONS PURE VANILLA EXTRACT

2 EGGS AT ROOM TEMPERATURE

3 CUPS ALMOND FLOUR

3/4 CUP COCOA POWDER

2 TEASPOONS CINNAMON

1/2 TEASPOON CAYENNE PEPPER

1/2 TEASPOON BAKING SODA

1/2 TEASPOON FINE SEA SALT

1 CUP ORGANIC DARK CHOCOLATE CHIPS

1    Preheat the oven to 350 degrees and line a baking pan with parchment paper.

2    Beat the butter, oil, sugar, date nectar, vanilla, and eggs together.

3    In a separate bowl combine the almond flour, cocoa powder, cinnamon, cayenne pepper, baking soda, and salt together.

4    Add the dry mixture to the wet ingredients 1/2 cup at a time. Stir in the chocolate chips.

5    Place the dough on the baking sheet using a melon ball scoop to keep the cookies even in size.

6    Bake 12–13 minutes.

7    Cool and enjoy.

# PUMPKIN SPICE COOKIES

*For family movie nights in the fall, we love to watch It's the Great Pumpkin, Charlie Brown. This is our cookie of choice then and anytime.*

1 1/2 CUPS ALMOND FLOUR

1 1/2 CUPS COCONUT SUGAR

2 TEASPOONS BAKING POWDER

1 TEASPOON CINNAMON

1 TEASPOON NUTMEG

1 TEASPOON CLOVE

1/2 TEASPOON ALLSPICE

8 OUNCES PLANT-BASED BUTTER AT ROOM TEMPERATURE

3/4 CUP COCONUT SUGAR

1/3 CUP MOLASSES

1 EGG

1 TEASPOON PURE VANILLA

1 CUP PUMPKIN PUREE

1  Preheat the oven to 325 degrees and line a large baking sheet with parchment paper.

2  Combine the almond flour, coconut sugar, baking powder, cinnamon, nutmeg, clove, and allspice in a large bowl.

3  In another large mixing bowl, beat the butter, coconut sugar and molasses together. Add the egg, vanilla, and pumpkin puree and beat for thirty more seconds.

4  With the mixer on low, slowly add the dry ingredients to the wet ingredients.

5  Using a melon ball scoop, arrange the cookies on the prepared baking sheet. Use a fork dipped in ice water to make a crisscross pattern on the cookie and to flatten them a bit. DO NOT flatten them all the way.

6  Bake for 13–14 minutes.

7  Cool completely before handling.

# OATMEAL RAISIN COOKIES

One of my favorite things about oatmeal cookies is their versatility. If you prefer, you can change out the raisins for dried cranberries, chocolate chips, nuts . . . the possibilities are endless!

4 TABLESPOONS PLANT-BASED BUTTER AT ROOM TEMPERATURE

1/4 CUP COCONUT OIL

3/4 CUP COCONUT SUGAR

2 TABLESPOONS DATE SYRUP

2 TEASPOONS PURE VANILLA EXTRACT

2 EGGS AT ROOM TEMPERATURE

3 CUPS ALMOND FLOUR

1/2 TEASPOON BAKING SODA

1/2 TEASPOON FINE SEA SALT

1 CUP GLUTEN-FREE OATS

1/2 CUP GOLDEN RAISINS

1   Preheat the oven to 350 degrees and line a baking pan with parchment paper.

2   Beat the butter, oil, sugar, date syrup, vanilla, and eggs together.

3   In a separate bowl, combine the almond flour, baking soda, and salt together.

4   Add the dry mixture to the wet ingredients 1/2 cup at a time. Stir in the oats and raisins.

5   Place the dough on the baking sheet using a melon ball scoop to keep the cookies even in size.

6   Bake 12-13 minutes.

7   Cool and enjoy.

HELPFUL TIP!  You can also freeze these cookies and take out just a few at a time!

# THUMBPRINT COOKIES

*You have never heard laughter like what will come out of the kitchen when you give your child permission to stick a finger in the cookie to make a hole! Isn't that what it is all about, fun?*

$\diamond\diamond\diamond\diamond\diamond\diamond\diamond\diamond\diamond\diamond\diamond\diamond\diamond\diamond\diamond\diamond\diamond\diamond\diamond\diamond\diamond\diamond\diamond\diamond\diamond\diamond\diamond\diamond\diamond\diamond\diamond\diamond\diamond\diamond\diamond\diamond\diamond\diamond\diamond\diamond\diamond\diamond\diamond\diamond$

2 3/4 CUPS ALMOND FLOUR

1/2 CUP PLANT-BASED BUTTER AT ROOM
    TEMPERATURE

1 1/2 CUPS COCONUT SUGAR

1 EGG AT ROOM TEMPERATURE

1 TEASPOON VANILLA

1 TEASPOON ALMOND EXTRACT

1/2 TEASPOON BAKING SODA

1/2 TEASPOON FINE SEA SALT

1/2 CUP OF JAM OR JELLY*

*My blueberry or strawberry preserves would be delicious with these cookies (see recipes on page <insert page number>)!

1    Preheat the oven to 350 degrees and line a baking sheet with parchment paper.

2    Combine all the ingredients, except the jam or jelly, in a large mixer. Scrape down the sides to make sure everything is incorporated.

3    Use a melon ball scoop to gather the dough and roll it into a ball. Arrange the cookies about 2 inches apart on the baking sheet. With a fork dipped in water, flatten the cookies a tiny bit. Make a "thumbprint" in the cookie and fill the hole with jam or jelly.

4    Bake for 15 minutes.

5    Cool and enjoy.

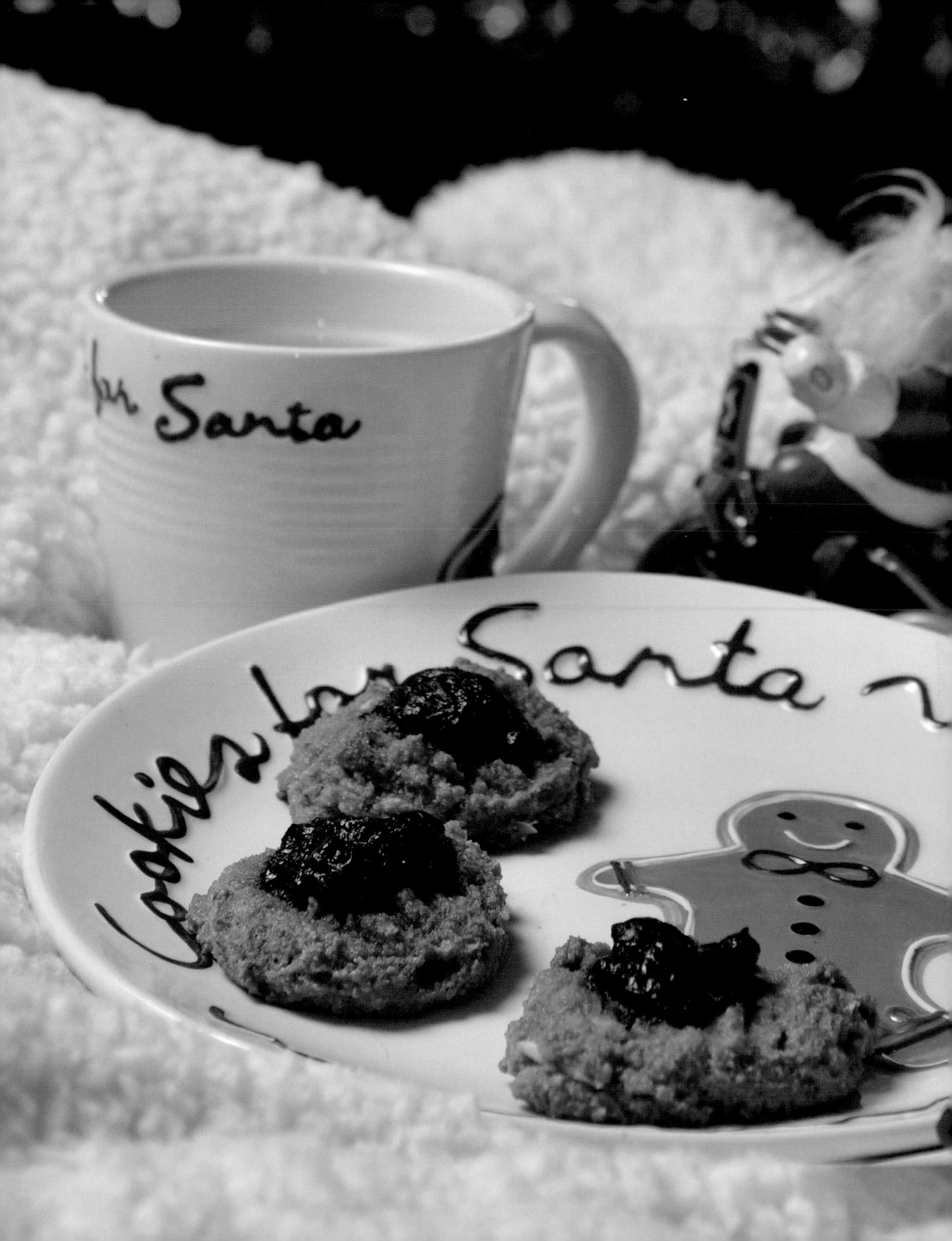
for Santa
Cookies for Santa

# OATMEAL, APRICOT, AND PISTACHIO COOKIES

*Dried fruits and nuts are great additions to any cookies. This combination of the sweet apricot and the nutty pistachios is one of my favorites.*

1 CUP ALMOND FLOUR

1/2 TEASPOON BAKING SODA

1/2 TEASPOON CINNAMON

1 CUP COCONUT SUGAR

1/2 PLANT-BASED BUTTER, MELTED

2 TEASPOONS VANILLA

1 EGG, BEATEN

1 1/2 CUPS GLUTEN-FREE OATS

1 CUP DRIED APRICOTS, UNSWEETENED AND ROUGHLY CHOPPED

1 CUP LIGHTLY SALTED AND ROASTED PISTACHIOS

1   Preheat the oven to 350 degrees and line a baking sheet with parchment paper.

2   Combine the almond flour, baking soda, cinnamon, and sugar in a large bowl.

3   Stir in the butter, vanilla, and egg. Stir the mixture well.

4   Add the oats, apricots, and pistachios last. Make sure they are all mixed in well.

5   Refrigerate the dough for one hour.

6   With a melon ball scoop, drop the cookie mixture about 2 inches apart onto the prepared baking sheet.

7   Bake the cookies for 10-12 minutes.

8   Cool and enjoy.

# PEANUT BUTTER COOKIES

*Beau loves anything with peanut butter. These cookies bring out a smile that tells you how delicious they are!*

1 CUP NATURAL PEANUT BUTTER (NO SUGAR ADDED)

2/3 CUP ALMOND FLOUR

1/2 TEASPOON BAKING SODA

1/2 CUP COCONUT SUGAR

1 TEASPOON PURE VANILLA EXTRACT

2 EGGS AT ROOM TEMPERATURE

1   Preheat the oven to 350 degrees and line a baking sheet with parchment paper.

2   Mix all ingredients together in a mixer.

3   Use a melon ball scoop to place the dough on the baking sheet. Use a fork dipped in water to flatten the cookies.

4   Bake the cookies for 10–12 minutes.

5   Cool and enjoy.

# BUTTER PECAN COOKIES

*Butter pecan ice cream was always my favorite, so I decided to make a cookie version to enjoy.*

## FOR THE BUTTERED PECANS

2 TABLESPOONS PLANT-BASED BUTTER                    2 CUPS CHOPPED PECANS

1   Melt the butter in a skillet over medium heat.

2   Add the chopped pecans and cook the pecans for 4–5 minutes, stirring occasionally.

3   Remove the pan from the heat and set aside.

## FOR THE COOKIE DOUGH

2 1/2 CUPS ALMOND FLOUR                    8 OUNCES PLANT-BASED BUTTER, MELTED

3 TABLESPOONS CORNSTARCH                   1 1/2 CUPS COCONUT SUGAR

1 TEASPOON SALT                           2 TEASPOONS PURE VANILLA EXTRACT

1 TEASPOON BAKING SODA                     2 EGGS AT ROOM TEMPERATURE

1   Preheat the oven to 375 degrees and line a baking sheet with parchment paper.

2   Combine ingredients in a mixer until the batter is smooth.

3   Fold in the buttered pecans.

4   Leaving room for the cookies to spread, drop the dough by the spoonful onto the baking sheet.

5   Bake for 10–12 minutes.

# COCONUT CREAM CHEESE SNOWBALLS

*In southern Georgia, we get snow once about every ten years, and even then it is usually very minimal. So if I can't make a real snowball, I will just make snowball cookies!*

8 OUNCES PLANT-BASED CREAM CHEESE AT ROOM TEMPERATURE

3/4 CUP PLANT-BASED BUTTER AT ROOM TEMPERATURE

1-1/2 CUPS COCONUT SUGAR

2 TEASPOONS PURE VANILLA EXTRACT

1/2 TEASPOON FINE SEA SALT

1/2 TEASPOON BAKING SODA

1 3/4 CUPS ALMOND FLOUR

1/2 CUP COCONUT FLOUR

2 CUPS SHREDDED COCONUT, UNSWEETENED

1   Preheat the oven to 375 degrees and line a baking sheet with parchment paper.

2   Fold together the cream cheese, butter, and coconut sugar in a large mixing bowl until the mixture is smooth.

3   Slowly mix in the remaining ingredients.

4   Use a melon ball scoop to drop the "snowballs" on the baking sheet.

5   Bake the cookies for 12–14 minutes.

6   Allow the cookies to cool for 10 minutes and then transfer them to a wire rack to cool completely before serving.

CHAPTER 2

—

# COBBLERS, BARS, AND BROWNIES

# BLUEBERRY COBBLER

*Every summer you can count on any variety from blueberry, blackberry, peach, and more. Blueberry has always been my favorite. For this cobbler, I added two of my favorite flavors, lemon and rosemary, to make it really amazing!*

## FOR THE COBBLER

- 3 CUPS FRESH BLUEBERRIES, WASHED AND DRAINED WELL
- 2 TABLESPOONS LEMON ZEST
- 1 TABLESPOON FRESH LEMON JUICE
- 2 TABLESPOONS CHOPPED FRESH ROSEMARY

1    Preheat the oven to 350 degrees and spray a 9x9 baking dish with non-stick spray.

2    In the baking dish, sprinkle the berries with the lemon zest, juice, and rosemary.

## FOR THE TOPPING

- 1 CUP ALMOND FLOUR
- 1/3 CUP COCONUT FLOUR
- 1 CUP COCONUT SUGAR
- 1 EGG, BEATEN
- 6 TABLESPOONS PLANT-BASED BUTTER, MELTED

1    In a separate bowl, combine the almond flour, coconut flour, coconut sugar, and egg. Pour this mixture over the berries.

2    Pour the melted butter evenly over the top and bake for 30 minutes or until golden brown.

# CHOCOLATE COBBLER

When I teach cooking classes, one of my favorite themes to do is to throw something at the students they don't expect. Classic fruit cobblers are, of course, amazing, but this chocolate twist is oh-so-good!

◇◇◇◇◇◇◇◇◇◇◇◇◇◇◇◇◇◇◇◇◇◇◇◇◇◇◇◇◇◇◇◇◇◇◇◇◇◇◇◇◇◇◇◇◇◇◇◇◇◇◇◇◇◇◇◇◇◇

## FOR THE COBBLER

1 CUP ALMOND FLOUR

1/2 CUP COCONUT FLOUR

2 TEASPOONS BAKING POWDER

3/4 CUP COCONUT SUGAR

1/2 CUP VANILLA ALMOND MILK, UNSWEETENED

1/3 CUP PLANT-BASED BUTTER, MELTED

1/4 TEASPOON SALT

1/4 CUP COCOA POWDER

2 TEASPOONS VANILLA EXTRACT

1/2 CUP DARK CHOCOLATE CHIPS

1   Preheat the oven to 350 degrees and grease an 8x8 baking dish with cooking spray.

2   Combine all ingredients together and pour into the baking dish.

## FOR THE TOPPING

1/2 CUP COCONUT SUGAR

1/4 CUP COCOA POWDER

1/3 CUP BOILING WATER

1   Combine the coconut sugar and cocoa powder and sprinkle it evenly over the cobbler mixture.

2   Pour the water evenly over the topping and DO NOT STIR!

3   Bake for 35–40 minutes.

4   Allow the cobbler to set for 10–15 minutes before serving.

# APPLE CREAM CHEESE COBBLER

*The perfect fall cobbler comes together with a cream cheese layer and classic fall spices.*

## FOR THE COBBLER

3 LARGE SWEET APPLES, CORED AND CUT INTO 8 LARGE SLICES*

1/2 CUP HONEY OR MAPLE SYRUP

2 PACKAGES (8 OUNCES EACH) PLANT-BASED CREAM CHEESE

*I like to use Honey Crisp or Gala apples.

1   Preheat the oven to 350 degrees and spray a 9x13 baking dish with cooking spray.

2   Arrange the apple slices in the bottom of the baking dish.

3   Whip the honey or maple syrup and cream cheese together until smooth and spread the mixture over the apples.

## FOR THE TOPPING

3 EGGS

2 CUPS ALMOND FLOUR

1/2 CUP COCONUT SUGAR

1 TEASPOON VANILLA

2 TEASPOONS CINNAMON

1 TEASPOON NUTMEG

1 TEASPOON BAKING SODA

1/2 TEASPOON FINE SEA SALT

1/2 CUP CHOPPED PECANS OR WALNUTS

1   Combine all ingredients together in a large bowl.

2   Pour the mixture over the apples and cream cheese mixture; bake for 45 minutes.

# MRS. JOY'S CONGO BARS

*My mother-in-law made these the first Christmas my husband and I were married. They are one of her many signature dishes!*

1/2 CUP COCONUT OIL

1 CUP COCONUT SUGAR

2 EGGS AT ROOM TEMPERATURE

2 TEASPOONS VANILLA

1 3/4 CUPS ALMOND FLOUR

1/2 TEASPOON BAKING SODA

1/2 TEASPOON FINE SEA SALT

1 CUP DAIRY-FREE AND REFINED SUGAR-FREE CHOCOLATE CHIPS

1  Preheat the oven to 350 degrees and grease a 9x13 baking pan.

2  Cream the oil, sugar, eggs, and vanilla together in a large bowl.

3  Add the flour, baking soda, salt, and chocolate chips and mix until completely incorporated.

4  Pour the mixture into the baking pan and bake for 25-30 minutes.

5  Cool for 15 minutes.

# BLONDIES

*My mom was known for making blondies when I was growing up. I think they were Daddy's favorite, and they were always at any family gathering.*

1/2 CUP DAIRY-FREE BUTTER AT ROOM TEMPERATURE

1 CUP COCONUT SUGAR

2 EGGS AT ROOM TEMPERATURE

2 TEASPOONS VANILLA

1 3/4 CUPS ALMOND FLOUR

1/2 TEASPOON BAKING SODA

1/2 TEASPOON FINE SEA SALT

1 TEASPOON CINNAMON

1 CUP CHOPPED PECANS

1   Preheat the oven to 350 degrees and grease a 9x13 baking pan.

2   Cream the butter, sugar, eggs, and vanilla together in a large bowl. Beat the mixture on high for about 2 minutes until fluffy.

3   Add the flour, baking soda, salt, and cinnamon; mix until completely incorporated. Stir in the pecans.

4   Pour the mixture into the baking pan and bake for 20-25 minutes.

5   Cool for 15 minutes.

# PECAN PIE GOOEY BARS

*A deliciously gooey handheld version of a pecan pie—need I say more? Yum!*

## FOR THE CRUST

1/2 CUP PLANT-BASED BUTTER, SOFTENED

1/4 CUP COCONUT SUGAR

1 CUP ALMOND FLOUR

2 TABLESPOONS COCONUT FLOUR

1   Preheat the oven to 350 degrees and grease an 8-inch cake pan with cooking spray.

2   Combine the butter, coconut sugar, almond flour, and coconut flour together in a small bowl. The texture will be crumbly.

3   Press the crust into the cake pan.

4   Bake the crust for 10 minutes and remove it from the oven.

## FOR THE TOPPING

1 CUP PURE MAPLE SYRUP

3/4 CUP COCONUT SUGAR

1/2 CUP CHOPPED PECANS

1/4 CUP PLANT-BASED BUTTER

2 EGGS

2 TABLESPOONS ALMOND FLOUR

1 TEASPOON PURE VANILLA

1   Combine the maple syrup, coconut sugar, and pecans in a saucepan and bring the mixture to a boil. Reduce the heat to low and cook for 4 minutes. Remove the mixture from the heat and stir in the butter.

2   In a small bowl, beat the eggs together with the almond flour and vanilla.

3   Whisk the egg mixture into the maple syrup mixture.

4   Pour the mixture over the crust and bake at 350 degrees for 25–30 minutes.

5   Cool completely before cutting.

# PB&J BARS

Almost everyone's childhood consisted of PB&Js; now I have turned them into a dessert! Go ahead and be a kid again! Feel free to substitute another nut butter if you prefer or need to because of a peanut allergy.

◇◇◇◇◇◇◇◇◇◇◇◇◇◇◇◇◇◇◇◇◇◇◇◇◇◇◇◇◇◇◇◇◇◇◇◇◇◇◇◇◇◇◇◇◇◇◇◇◇◇◇◇◇◇◇◇◇◇◇◇◇

3/4 CUP NATURAL PEANUT BUTTER (NO SUGAR ADDED)

1/2 CUP COCONUT SUGAR

1 TEASPOON VANILLA

2 CUPS ALMOND FLOUR

1/2 TEASPOON BAKING SODA

1/2 TEASPOON FINE SEA SALT

12 OUNCES JAM OR JELLY*

I like to use my strawberry or blueberry preserves with these cookies (see recipes on page <insert page number>)!

1   Preheat the oven to 350 degrees and spray an 8x11 baking dish with cooking spray.

2   Cream the eggs, peanut butter, coconut sugar, and vanilla together.

3   Add the almond flour, baking soda, and salt to the mixture and mix well.

4   Pour the peanut butter mixture into the pan. Wet your hands slightly with water and press the mixture evenly into the bottom of the pan.

5   Spoon the fruit spread onto the peanut butter mixture and spread it evenly across the top; bake for 22–25 minutes.

6   Cool completely before serving.

DECORATING IDEA! For an extra crunch, add chopped peanuts to the top before serving!

# TOFFEE BARS

*The ultimate in a homemade candy bar: sweet, salty, and chocolaty all in one!*

1 CUP DAIRY-FREE BUTTER

1 EGG YOLK

1 CUP COCONUT SUGAR

1 CUP ALMOND FLOUR

1/4 CUP COCONUT FLOUR

1 TEASPOON VANILLA

2 CUPS REFINED SUGAR-FREE CHOCOLATE CHIPS

1/2 CUP CHOPPED SALTED AND TOASTED PECANS

1   Preheat the oven to 325 degrees and grease a 9x13 baking pan.

2   Cream the butter, egg yolk, and coconut sugar together; mix well. Add the almond flour, coconut flour, and vanilla, beating until well mixed.

3   Spread the mixture in the baking pan and bake for 25 minutes.

4   Remove the pan from the oven and spread the chocolate chips over the hot crust. Once the chips are melted, sprinkle the pecans over the chocolate.

5   Allow the bars to cool completely and harden before cutting.

# PUMPKIN PECAN OATMEAL BARS

*This is the perfect fully loaded fall breakfast bar. Make these up over the weekend for a quick breakfast as you head out the door or for an after-school snack.*

1/2 CUP PUMPKIN PUREE

1 EGG

1 CUP VANILLA ALMOND MILK, UNSWEETENED

1 CUP PECAN OIL

1 CUP COCONUT SUGAR

1/2 TEASPOON BAKING POWDER

1 TEASPOON SALT

1 TEASPOON CINNAMON

1 TEASPOON CLOVE

1 TEASPOON NUTMEG

1 TEASPOON VANILLA

2 1/4 CUPS GLUTEN-FREE OATS

3/4 CUP CHOPPED PECANS

1     Preheat the oven to 350 degrees and spray an 8x8 baking pan with non-stick cooking spray.

2     Whisk together the pumpkin puree, egg, almond milk, and oil.

3     Stir in the remaining ingredients, making sure to mix well.

4     Pour the mixture into the baking pan and bake for 35–40 minutes.

# DOUBLE CHOCOLATE BROWNIES

*The more chocolate, the better they are! These brownies are rich and super delicious.*

5 EGGS

1/2 CUP COCOA POWDER

1 CUP HONEY

1/2 TEASPOON BAKING SODA

1/2 CUP COCONUT FLOUR

1/8 TEASPOON FINE SEA SALT

1/3 CUP COCONUT OIL

2 TEASPOONS WATER

1 CUP CHOCOLATE CHIPS

1 CUP CHOPPED PECANS

1    Preheat the oven to 350 degrees and grease an 8x8 baking pan.

2    Combine all ingredients together in a large bowl or mixer.

3    Pour the batter into the baking pan and bake for 25-30 minutes.

CHAPTER 3

———

CAKES

# ORANGE CHIFFON CAKE

## FOR THE CAKE

2 1/2 CUPS ALMOND FLOUR

1/2 CUP COCONUT FLOUR

5 EGGS AT ROOM TEMPERATURE, BEATEN

1/2 CUP COCONUT OIL

1/2 CUP FRESH ORANGE JUICE

ZEST OF 2 ORANGES

ZEST OF 1 LEMON

1 TABLESPOON BAKING POWDER

1 TEASPOON FINE SEA SALT

1 CUP COCONUT SUGAR

1   Preheat the oven to 350 degrees and spray a Bundt pan with cooking spray.

2   Combine all ingredients in a large bowl. Be sure to mix the ingredients well.

3   Pour the batter into the Bundt pan and bake the cake for 40-45 minutes.

4   Cool completely before icing.

## FOR THE ICING

1 CUP PLANT-BASED BUTTER, SOFTENED

1 CUP POWDERED COCONUT SUGAR

2 TABLESPOONS ORANGE ZEST

1 TEASPOON LEMON ZEST

1   Beat the butter and powdered coconut sugar together until smooth. Stir in the zests.

After icing the cake, you can serve as is or with my favorite: a little shaved dark chocolate!

# APPLE SPICE CAKE

This is one of the easiest cakes you will ever make. It is just as good for breakfast as it is for dessert!

2 CUPS ALMOND FLOUR

1 CUP COCONUT SUGAR

1 TEASPOON BAKING SODA

1/2 TEASPOON FINE SEA SALT

2 TEASPOONS CINNAMON

1 TEASPOON NUTMEG

2 CUPS OF SWEET APPLE, SHREDDED*

3 EGGS AT ROOM TEMPERATURE, BEATEN

1 TEASPOON VANILLA

1   Preheat the oven to 350 degrees and grease an 8x8 cake pan.

2   Combine the almond flour, coconut sugar, baking soda, salt, cinnamon, and nutmeg in a large bowl.

3   Add the apples, eggs, and vanilla to the dry ingredients and mix well.

4   Pour the mixture into the prepared cake pan and bake for 30-35 minutes.

*I like to use Gala apples for this recipe.

# PEANUT BUTTER BANANA COFFEE CAKE

*My peanut butter banana cake—with its crumbly topping—is a must for any peanut butter fan. The crunchy surprise of the chopped peanuts inside the cake give it an unusual and delicious crunch.*

## FOR THE CAKE

1/4 CUP COCONUT OIL, MELTED

1/4 CUP MAPLE SYRUP

1 TEASPOON VANILLA

4 EGGS AT ROOM TEMPERATURE

2 RIPE BANANAS

1/2 CUP COCONUT SUGAR

1/4 CUP COCONUT FLOUR

1 CUP ALMOND FLOUR

1/2 CUP CHOPPED PEANUTS

1/2 TEASPOON BAKING SODA

1/2 TEASPOON SALT

1   Preheat the oven to 325 degrees and spray a 9x9 baking dish with non-stick spray.

2   In a large mixing bowl, combine the wet ingredients and mix well. Slowly add the dry ingredients and mix well.

3   Pour into the greased pan.

## FOR THE TOPPING

1/4 CUP COCONUT FLOUR

1/2 CUP ALMOND FLOUR

2 TABLESPOONS COCONUT SUGAR

3 TABLESPOONS NATURAL PEANUT BUTTER

1 TABLESPOON COCONUT OIL

1   Combine all the ingredients in a bowl and stir well with a fork.

2   Pour the topping over the cake mixture and bake for 45 minutes.

VARIATION! You can omit the peanuts and peanut butter and add dark chocolate cocoa chips to the batter for a chocolate banana cake!

# GERMAN CHOCOLATE CAKE

One of the most iconic and beloved cakes of all time was first introduced in 1957 by Mrs. George Clay. Since then, it has been on magazine covers and at holiday gatherings all over the world.

## FOR THE CAKE

8 EGGS

1 CUP HONEY

2 CUPS ALMOND FLOUR

1 TEASPOON BAKING SODA

1 CUP COCOA POWDER

1 TEASPOON FINE SEA SALT

1 TABLESPOON VANILLA

2 TABLESPOONS COCONUT OIL

1   Preheat the oven to 350 degrees and grease two round cake pans.

2   Mix all ingredients together in a large bowl or mixer.

3   Divide the batter evenly between the two cake pans and bake for 25–30 minutes.

4   Cool before frosting.

## FOR THE ICING

1 CAN (13.5 OUNCES) COCONUT MILK

1 1/2 CUPS COCONUT SUGAR

3/4 CUP PLANT-BASED BUTTER

6 EGG YOLKS, LIGHTLY BEATEN

1 1/2 TEASPOONS VANILLA

2 CUPS SHREDDED COCONUT, UNSWEETENED

2 CUPS TOASTED PECANS

1   Cook the coconut milk, coconut sugar, butter, egg yolks, and vanilla together in a saucepan over medium heat until the butter melts and the sugar dissolves. Cook, stirring constantly, for 8–10 minutes until the mixture thickens and has a thin pudding-like thickness. Stir in the coconut and pecans.

2   Allow the mixture to cool for 45 minutes, stirring every 15 minutes, before frosting the cake.

# HONEY CAKE

*One day when Dylan was about three years old, we had just watched the Winnie the Pooh movie. He then decided that I needed to make a cake that "Pooh" would like.*

## FOR THE CAKE

2 CUPS ALMOND FLOUR

1/2 TEASPOON BAKING SODA

1 TEASPOON FINE SEA SALT

1 TEASPOON CINNAMON

1 TABLESPOON ORANGE ZEST

3 EGGS

3/4 CUP COCONUT OIL

3/4 CUP COCONUT SUGAR

1/4 CUP ALMOND MILK

1 CUP WALNUTS, CHOPPED

1   Preheat the oven to 350 degrees and grease a 9x9 baking pan.

2   Combine the flour, baking soda, salt, cinnamon, and orange zest in a large bowl.

3   In a separate bowl, whisk the eggs together and add the coconut oil, coconut sugar, and almond milk.

4   Combine the wet ingredients with the dry ingredients and mix well. Stir in the chopped walnuts.

5   Pour the batter into the baking pan and bake for 35 minutes.

6   Cool the cake for 15 minutes while you prepare the honey glaze.

## FOR THE GLAZE

1 CUP HONEY

3/4 CUP WATER

1 CUP COCONUT SUGAR

1 TEASPOON LEMON JUICE

1   In a saucepan, combine the honey, water, and sugar. Bring the mixture to a simmer and cook for 5 minutes. Stir in the lemon juice and bring to a boil for 2 minutes.

2   Pour the glaze over the cake.

# CARROT CUPCAKES

*This is an absolute must at the table for Easter. I like to add a little color by using purple and orange carrots!*

## FOR THE CUPCAKES

3/4 CUP COCONUT OIL

1 CUP COCONUT SUGAR

3 EGGS AT ROOM TEMPERATURE

1 TEASPOON PURE VANILLA

1 CUP CRUSHED PINEAPPLE (NO ADDED SUGAR, DRAINED WELL, AND RESERVE 1 TABLESPOON JUICE)

1 CUP GRATED CARROT

1 1/3 CUPS ALMOND FLOUR

1 TEASPOON BAKING SODA

1 TEASPOON FINE SEA SALT

2 TEASPOONS CINNAMON

1 1/2 TEASPOONS GROUND GINGER

1 CUP CHOPPED WALNUTS

1   Preheat the oven to 350 degrees and spray a muffin tin with cooking spray.

2   Cream the coconut oil, coconut sugar, and eggs together in a large bowl. Add the vanilla, pineapple, and carrots.

3   In a separate bowl, mix the almond flour, baking soda, salt, cinnamon, and ginger together. Add to the wet ingredients. Stir in the walnuts last.

4   Pour the mixture into the prepared baking pan and bake for 25 minutes.

5   Cool completely before icing.

## FOR THE ICING

8 OUNCES PLANT-BASED CREAM CHEESE

1/2 CUP HONEY

1/2 CUP COCONUT SUGAR

2 TEASPOONS PURE VANILLA

1 TABLESPOON RESERVED PINEAPPLE JUICE

1   Whip together all ingredients.

2   Keep the icing chilled until ready to ice the cake.

# COLA CAKE

*This is a fun cake! Nostalgia at its best! As a side note, this was my grandmother Mimi's tablecloth that she used for all of her bridge parties.*

## FOR THE CAKE

2 CUPS ALMOND FLOUR

2 CUPS COCONUT SUGAR

1 TEASPOON BAKING SODA

1/2 TEASPOON CINNAMON

1/2 TEASPOON FINE SEA SALT

1 CUP PLANT-BASED BUTTER AT ROOM

TEMPERATURE

1 CAN (12 OUNCES) ZEVIA COLA

1/4 CUP COCOA POWDER, UNSWEETENED

1/2 CUP ALMOND MILK

2 EGGS, BEATEN

1 TEASPOON VANILLA

1   Preheat the oven to 350 degrees and spray a 9x13 baking pan with non-stick cooking spray.

2   In a large bowl, combine the flour, sugar, baking soda, cinnamon, and salt.

3   In a saucepan, over medium-high heat, stir the butter, cola, and cocoa powder together. Stir until the butter is melted and the cocoa powder is incorporated.

4   Pour the cola mixture in with the dry ingredients. Stir in the almond milk, eggs, and vanilla.

5   Pour the cake into the prepared baking and bake for 35-40 minutes.

## FOR THE ICING

1/2 CUP PLANT-BASED BUTTER

1 CAN (12 OUNCES) ZEVIA COLA

1/2 CUP DARK CHOCOLATE

1/4  COCOA POWDER, UNSWEETENED

4 CUPS POWDERED COCONUT SUGAR

1   Heat the butter and cola together over medium heat. Once the butter is melted, turn off the heat and stir in the chocolate to melt. Last, whisk in the cocoa powder and powdered coconut sugar.

2   Pour the icing over the cake while the cake is warm.

# LEMON COCONUT CUPCAKES

## FOR THE CUPCAKES

3/4 CUP ALMOND FLOUR

3/4 CUP COCONUT FLOUR

1/2 TEASPOON FINE SALT

1 1/2 TEASPOONS BAKING POWDER

3/4 CUP SHREDDED COCONUT, UNSWEETENED

1 CUP PLANT-BASED BUTTER, MELTED

1/2 CUP COCONUT OIL

1/2 CUP COCONUT SUGAR

3 EGGS AT ROOM TEMPERATURE, BEATEN

3 TABLESPOONS LEMON JUICE

1/2 CUP HONEY

2 TABLESPOONS LEMON ZEST

1   Preheat the oven to 350 degrees and line eight muffin tins with paper liners.

2   In a large bowl, combine the almond flour, coconut flour, salt, baking powder, and coconut.

3   In a separate bowl, whisk the butter, oil, sugar, eggs, lemon juice, and honey together.

4   Add the wet ingredients to the dry and stir in the lemon zest.

5   Divide the batter evenly between the eight tins and bake for 20–25 minutes.

6   Cool completely before frosting.

## FOR THE ICING

8 OUNCES PLANT-BASED CREAM CHEESE

1/4 CUP HONEY

1/2 CUP POWDERED COCONUT SUGAR

1 TABLESPOON LEMON JUICE

1 TABLESPOON LEMON ZEST

ADDITIONAL COCONUT FOR GARNISH

1   Using a hand mixer or stand mixer, cream the cream cheese and honey together. Slowly add the powdered coconut sugar, lemon juice, and lemon zest. You may need to add more powdered coconut sugar to get the right consistency depending on what brand of plant-based cheese you use.

2   Frost the cupcakes and sprinkle with extra coconut.

VARIATION! You can make this cake in a 9x5 loaf pan lined with parchment paper and cooking spray and bake it for 45–50 minutes

# FIG UPSIDE-DOWN CAKE

## FOR THE TOPPING

4 TABLESPOONS PLANT-BASED BUTTER

1/2 CUP COCONUT SUGAR

2 TABLESPOONS MAPLE SYRUP

20 SMALL FIGS, WASHED AND CUT IN HALF

1   Preheat the oven to 350 degrees and spray the bottom of a cast-iron skillet with non stick cooking spray.

2   Combine the butter, coconut sugar, and maple syrup together in a saucepan over medium heat until the sugar is dissolved.

3   Arrange the figs in the bottom of the cast-iron skillet.

4   Pour the warm mixture over the figs.

## FOR THE CAKE

1 1/2 CUPS ALMOND FLOUR

1 1/2 TEASPOONS BAKING POWDER

1/2 TEASPOON SALT

1 TEASPOON VANILLA

2 EGGS AT ROOM TEMPERATURE

1/2 CUP PLANT-BASED MILK

1   Combine all ingredients in a large bowl.

2   Pour the mixture over the figs and bake the cake for 40–45 minutes.

3   Allow the cake to cool for 15 minutes before turning the cake out onto a plate.

# PUMPKIN GINGERSNAP CHEESECAKE

*Take Thanksgiving to a whole new level! Two of my favorite recipes all in one, pumpkin and cheesecake. This recipe will be a perfectly delicious showstopper.*

## FOR THE CRUST

2 1/2 CUPS GINGERSNAP COOKIE CRUMBS (SEE GINGER COOKIE RECIPE ON PAGE 6)

2/3 CUP PLANT-BASED BUTTER, MELTED

1/2 CUP COCONUT SUGAR

1  Preheat the oven to 350 degrees (if using a dark-coated pan, reduce the heat to 325 degrees) and grease a cheesecake pan.

2  Combine the cookie crumbs, butter, and coconut sugar in a small bowl.

3  Press the mixture into the bottom and slightly up the sides of the prepared pan.

## FOR THE FILLING

1 1/2 CUPS PUMPKIN PUREE

3 LARGE EGGS

3 PACKAGES (8 OUNCES EACH) PLANT-BASED CREAM CHEESE

1 1/2 TEASPOONS CINNAMON

1/2 TEASPOON GINGER

1/2 TEASPOON NUTMEG, PLUS GARNISH

11 CUPS COCONUT SUGAR

2 TABLESPOONS COCONUT CREAM, PLUS GARNISH

1 TEASPOON VANILLA

1  Beat together the pumpkin, eggs, and cream cheese until smooth. Mix in the cinnamon, ginger, nutmeg, and coconut sugar. With the mixer on low, slowly add the coconut cream and vanilla. Increase the speed to medium and mix until all is well blended.

2  Pour the mixture over the crust and bake for 1 hour.

3  Allow the cake to cool completely and then chill for 3 hours.

4  Garnish with whipped coconut cream and nutmeg.

CHAPTER 4

—

# MUFFINS AND BREADS

# PUMPKIN CRANBERRY NUT BREAD

*What do you want to eat with your coffee or tea while you watch the Macy's Day Parade on Thanksgiving morning? (Hint, hint: It's this!)*

3 CUPS ALMOND FLOUR

1 TEASPOON FINE SEA SALT

1 TEASPOON BAKING SODA

1 TEASPOON BAKING POWDER

1 TEASPOON GROUND CLOVE

2 TEASPOONS GROUND CINNAMON

1 1/3 CUPS COCONUT SUGAR

2 CUPS PUMPKIN PUREE (NOT PIE FILLING)

1/2 CUP APPLESAUCE, UNSWEETENED

1/2 COCONUT OIL

1 TEASPOON PURE VANILLA EXTRACT

1 CUP DRIED CRANBERRIES

1 CUP CHOPPED PECANS OR WALNUTS

1   Preheat the oven to 350 degrees and grease two 8x4 loaf pans with non-stick spray.

2   In a large bowl, whisk together the almond flour, salt, baking soda, baking powder, clove, cinnamon, and coconut sugar.

3   In a separate bowl, combine the pumpkin puree, applesauce, coconut oil, and vanilla.

4   Mix the wet ingredients into the dry ingredients; mix well.

5   Fold the cranberries and nuts into the mixture.

6   Pour the batter into the prepared loaf pans and bake for 45–50 minutes.

HELPFUL TIP! To make the biscotti, allow the bread to cool completely. Slice the cooled bread into 1/2-inch slices and arrange on a parchment paper—lined baking sheet. Bake at 350 degrees for 10–12 minutes. Using a spatula, flip the slices over to the other side and bake for an additional 10–12 minutes.

# GINGERBREAD

*Bring on the caroling party with this holiday classic! This is delicious just as it is, but I love to serve it over-the-top for Christmas with lemon curd and a drizzle of warm vanilla almond milk.*

2 CUPS ALMOND FLOUR ·

1/2 TEASPOON BAKING SODA

1/2 TEASPOON BAKING POWDER

1/4 TEASPOON FINE SEA SALT

2 TEASPOONS GINGER

1 TEASPOON CINNAMON

1/4 TEASPOON GROUND CLOVE

1/2 CUP COCONUT SUGAR

2 EGGS

1/2 CUP MOLASSES

1/4 CUP COCONUT OIL

1   Preheat the oven to 350 degrees and spray an 8x8 baking dish with non-stick cooking spray.

2   Combine the dry ingredients in a large bowl.

3   Whisk together the eggs, molasses, and oil. Combine the dry and wet ingredients.

4   Pour the batter into the prepared baking dish and bake for 30 minutes.

# OATMEAL BLUEBERRY ALMOND MUFFINS

*This is a delicious twist on a blueberry muffin with oats and almonds. This oat-packed muffin makes a great breakfast for busy school mornings.*

2 1/4 CUPS GLUTEN-FREE OATS

1 CUP ALMOND FLOUR

1 TEASPOON BAKING POWDER

1/2 TEASPOON FINE SEA SALT

1 3/4 CUPS VANILLA ALMOND MILK, UNSWEETENED

2 EGGS

1 CUP COCONUT SUGAR

1 TEASPOON ALMOND FLAVORING

1/2 CUP SLIVERED ALMONDS

1 CUP FRESH BLUEBERRIES

1   Preheat the oven to 350 degrees and prepare sixteen muffin cups with paper liners.

2   Combine all ingredients except the blueberries in a large bowl mixing. Once the batter is combined, gently fold in the blueberries.

3   Fill the muffin cups evenly with the batter and bake for 18–20 minutes.

# BANANA CHOCOLATE CHIP MUFFINS

*Oh yes! These delicious muffins will have everyone singing your praises on Saturday morning. You can make regular-size muffins or mini muffins, which are perfect for school treats!*

3 RIPE BANANAS

3 EGGS

1/2 CUP COCONUT SUGAR

1 TEASPOON VANILLA

1/2 TEASPOON BAKING SODA

1/2 TEASPOON FINE SEA SALT

3 CUPS ALMOND FLOUR

1 CUP CHOCOLATE CHIPS

1   Preheat the oven to 350 degrees and prepare twelve muffin cups with paper liners.

2   In a mixer, combine the bananas, eggs, coconut sugar, and vanilla together.

3   Combine the dry ingredients—except for the chocolate chips—in a separate bowl.

4   Slowly add the dry ingredients to the wet ingredients. Stir in the chocolate chips.

5   Pour the mixture evenly into the muffin cups and bake for 12-15 minutes.

# CINNAMON PECAN MUFFINS

*This Georgia girl is always looking for something else to add pecans to. Cinnamon and pecan muffins make the perfect combination. Sometimes I will add a few golden raisins, cranberries, or even chocolate chips!*

1 1/2 CUPS ALMOND FLOUR

1 1/2 TEASPOONS BAKING POWDER

1 TEASPOON BAKING SODA

1/4 TEASPOON FINE SEA SALT

2 1/2 TEASPOONS CINNAMON

3/4 CUP COCONUT SUGAR

1 TEASPOON VANILLA

1 EGG, BEATEN

2/3 CUP PLANT-BASED BUTTER, MELTED

1/3 CUP VANILLA ALMOND MILK, UNSWEETENED

1/2 CUP CHOPPED PECANS

1   Preheat the oven to 350 degrees and prepare twelve muffin cups with paper liners.

2   Combine all ingredients—except the pecans—in a large bowl, mixing well to make sure everything is well blended. Stir in the pecans.

3   Divide the batter evenly among the muffin cups and bake for 12–14 minutes.

# PEACH COBBLER MUFFINS

*In the summer, there is absolutely nothing like a sweet Georgia peach! We make cobblers, ice cream, and preserves with them. This is my twist on a way to have dessert for breakfast with my peach cobbler muffins!*

## FOR THE MUFFIN

1 CUP ALMOND FLOUR

1/4 CUP COCONUT FLOUR

1/2 TEASPOON FINE SEA SALT

2/3 CUP COCONUT SUGAR

1/2 CUP VANILLA ALMOND MILK, UNSWEETENED

1 EGG

1/4 CUP COCONUT OIL

2 CUPS CHOPPED FRESH PEACHES

1   Preheat the oven to 350 degrees and prepare twelve muffin cups with paper liners.

2   Combine the almond flour, coconut flour, salt, and sugar in a bowl; make sure it is well blended.

3   In a smaller bowl, whisk together the almond milk, egg, and coconut oil.

4   Pour the wet-ingredient mixture over the dry ingredients and mix well. Stir in the peaches.

## FOR THE TOPPING

1/4 CUP COCONUT FLOUR

1/2 CUP ALMOND FLOUR

2 TABLESPOONS COCONUT SUGAR

1/2 TEASPOON CINNAMON

3 TABLESPOONS HONEY

1 TABLESPOON COCONUT OIL

1   Combine the ingredients in a bowl to form a crumbly mixture.

2   Divide the muffin mixture evenly among the muffin cups. Divide the streusel mixture evenly on top of the muffin mixture.

3   Bake for 13–15 minutes.

# BANANA NUT BREAD

*Banana Bread climbed to popularity during the Great Depression. During those days, nothing was allowed to go to waste, not even a banana. By the 1930s, banana bread recipes began popping up in magazines everywhere, including Better Homes and Gardens.*

◇◇◇◇◇◇◇◇◇◇◇◇◇◇◇◇◇◇◇◇◇◇◇◇◇◇◇◇◇◇◇◇◇◇◇◇◇◇◇◇◇◇◇◇◇◇◇◇◇◇◇◇◇◇◇◇◇◇◇◇◇◇◇◇◇◇◇◇

3 RIPE BANANAS

2 EGGS

1/2 CUP HONEY

1 TEASPOON PURE VANILLA EXTRACT

2 TABLESPOONS COCONUT SUGAR

3 CUPS ALMOND FLOUR

1/2 TEASPOON FINE SEA SALT

1 TEASPOON BAKING SODA

1/2 CUP CHOPPED WALNUTS

1   Preheat the oven to 325 degrees and spray a loaf pan with non-stick cooking spray.

2   In a mixer, combine the bananas, eggs, honey, vanilla, and coconut sugar together.

3   In a separate bowl, combine the almond flour, salt, and baking soda.

4   Slowly add the dry ingredients to the wet ingredients. Stir in the walnuts.

5   Pour the mixture into the prepared pan and bake for 50–55 minutes.

6   Cool the bread in the pan for 5 minutes before turning it out onto a board to finish cooling.

VARIATIONS!  You can substitute pecans for the walnuts, if you prefer, and even add 1/2 cup dark chocolate chips!
For muffins, use lined baking cups and reduce cooking time to 20–22 minutes.

CHAPTER 5

—

PIES

# ALMOND FLOUR PIE CRUST

*Talk about easy! This pie crust is so simple and is a "no fail" start to the perfect pie.*

1/4 CUP COCONUT OIL

1/4 CUP PLANT-BASED BUTTER, MELTED

1 CUP ALMOND FLOUR

1 CUP COCONUT FLOUR

1/2 TEASPOON FINE SEA SALT

1 EGG AT ROOM TEMPERATURE

1    Preheat the oven to 375 degrees and spray a 9-inch pie plate with non-stick cooking spray.

2    Mix all ingredients together.

3    Press the mixture into the pie plate and bake for 12–15 minutes.

4    Cool completely and fill with your favorite filling.

# DEATH BY CHOCOLATE PIE FILLING

*I am a firm believer that every day should contain chocolate! The hardest part about this recipe is waiting for it to cool so you can have a slice!*

◇◇◇◇◇◇◇◇◇◇◇◇◇◇◇◇◇◇◇◇◇◇◇◇◇◇◇◇◇◇◇◇◇◇◇◇◇◇◇◇◇◇◇◇◇◇◇◇◇◇◇◇◇◇◇◇◇◇◇◇◇◇◇◇◇◇◇◇◇◇◇◇◇◇◇◇◇◇

## FOR THE CRUST

1 ALMOND FLOUR PIE CRUST, PREPARED AND COOLED

1    See page 80.

## FOR THE FILLING

4 EGG YOLKS

3 CUPS VANILLA ALMOND MILK, UNSWEETENED

2/3 CUP COCONUT SUGAR

1/3 CUP CORNSTARCH

1 TEASPOON PURE VANILLA EXTRACT

1/2 TEASPOON FINE SEA SALT

2 CUPS HU KITCHEN CHOCOLATE GEMS

2 TABLESPOONS PLANT-BASED BUTTER

1    In a small bowl, combine the egg yolks and almond milk.

2    In a two-quart saucepan, stir together the coconut sugar and cornstarch. Pour in the egg and milk mixture, blending together over medium heat—stirring constantly—until the mixture comes to a low boil. Boil the mixture for 1 minute or until it begins to thicken. Remove the mixture from the heat.

3    Stir in the vanilla, salt, chocolate gems, and butter until the chocolate is melted and the mixture is smooth.

4    Pour into the pie crust and cover with plastic wrap.

5    Cool completely and then place in the refrigerator for several hours until firm before cutting.

# BEAU'S PEANUT BUTTER PIE FILLING

*My "Beau Man" would rather have this pie for his birthday than a cake. It takes no time to whip up and will definitely be a family favorite!*

## FOR THE CRUST

1 CHOCOLATE PIE CRUST, PREPARED AND COOLED

1   See page 82.

## FOR THE FILLING

1 CUP NATURAL PEANUT BUTTER (NO SUGAR ADDED)

8 OUNCES PLANT-BASED CREAM CHEESE

3/4 CUP COCONUT SUGAR

1 CUP COCONUT CREAM, WHIPPED

1 TEASPOON VANILLA

CHOPPED PEANUTS, FOR GARNISH

1   Combine the peanut butter, cream cheese, and coconut sugar in a mixing bowl; mix until smooth. Fold in the whipped coconut cream.

2   Pour the mixture into the pie crust and garnish with chopped peanuts.

# CRUSTLESS COCONUT PIE

*Growing up, I always loved the coconut and chocolate balls my mother would make at Christmas. This is my idea of what a pie with the same components would be!*

1 CUP COCONUT MILK

1/4 CUP PLANT-BASED BUTTER

1/2 CUP DAIRY- AND REFINED SUGAR-FREE CHOCOLATE CHIPS

1 CUP SHREDDED COCONUT, UNSWEETENED

1 CUP COCONUT SUGAR

1/2 CUP COCONUT FLOUR

1/4 CUP ALMOND FLOUR

1 TEASPOON VANILLA

1 TEASPOON ALMOND EXTRACT

3 EGGS, BEATEN

1  Preheat the oven to 350 degrees and spray a deep-dish pie plate with non-stick cooking spray.

2  Combine the coconut milk, butter, and chocolate chips in a saucepan over medium heat, stirring often, until the butter and chocolate are melted. Remove the pan from the heat and stir in the remaining ingredients until smooth.

3  Pour the mixture into the pie plate and bake for 45 minutes, or until the center is set.

4  Cool completely and chill for 2–3 hours before serving.

# LEMON BLUEBERRY PIE

*When my husband and I lived in Tifton, Georgia, for a couple of years we had blueberry bushes for the first time. The blueberries were so plentiful, I think we ate blueberries every day in the summers, and we froze even more!*

## FOR THE CRUST

1 COCONUT FLOUR PIE CRUST, PREPARED AND COOLED

1    See page 83.

## FOR THE TOPPING

2 PINTS FRESH BLUEBERRIES, DIVIDED

1/4 CUP COCONUT SUGAR

2 TABLESPOONS HONEY

1 TABLESPOON WATER

1 TABLESPOON CORNSTARCH MIXED WITH 1 TABLESPOON WATER

2 TEASPOONS LEMON ZEST

2 TEASPOONS LEMON JUICE

1    Combine half of the blueberries with the coconut sugar, honey, and water in a saucepan over medium heat. Stir the mixture constantly to prevent it from burning. Once the berries begin to break down, the sugar is dissolved, and the mixture begins to boil, pour in the cornstarch/water mixture. The mixture will thicken for about a minute. Remove from the heat.

2    Add the remaining blueberries, lemon zest, and lemon juice, stirring well.

3    Chill in the refrigerator until completely cool.

## FOR THE FILLING

8 OUNCES PLANT-BASED CREAM CHEESE

1/2 TEASPOON VANILLA

1 CUP POWDERED COCONUT SUGAR

1 CUP COCONUT CREAM, WHIPPED

1    In a large bowl, whip the cream cheese, vanilla, and powdered coconut sugar together. Carefully fold in the whipped coconut cream until smooth.

2    Spoon the mixture into the pie crust and top with blueberry topping. Chill for 2 hours before serving.

# GEORGIA PECAN-CRUSTED PUMPKIN PIE

## FOR THE CRUST

2 CUPS PECANS

2 TABLESPOONS PLANT-BASED BUTTER, MELTED

4 TABLESPOONS COCONUT SUGAR

1/2 TEASPOON VANILLA

1 TEASPOON VANILLA

1  Preheat the oven to 325 degrees and spray a 9-inch pie pan with non-stick cooking spray.

2  In a food processor, grind the pecans until fine. Add the butter, coconut sugar, and vanilla until the crust begins to roll up the sides of the food processor.

3  Press the mixture into the pie pan and bake for 15–20 minutes.

4  Allow the crust to cool completely.

## FOR THE PIE

8 OUNCES PLANT-BASED CREAM CHEESE

1 CUP CANNED PUMPKIN PUREE

1/2 CUP COCONUT SUGAR

1 TEASPOON FRESH NUTMEG, GRATED

1 TEASPOON GROUND CINNAMON

2 CUPS COCONUT CREAM

1 TEASPOON VANILLA

1  Combine the cream cheese, pumpkin, coconut sugar, nutmeg, and cinnamon.

2  In a separate bowl, whip the coconut cream with the vanilla.

3  Fold 2/3 of the whipped cream mixture in with the cream cheese mixture and pour into the cooled crust.

4  Top the pie with the remaining whipped cream.

5  Chill for 3–4 hours before serving.

CHAPTER 6

—

# THE SAVORY SIDE OF THINGS

# PARMESAN CHEESE STRAWS

*Party-perfect cheese straws every time! I love to serve these plain or topped with a bit of homemade pepper jelly.*

1 CUP ALMOND FLOUR, PACKED TIGHT

1/4 CUP COCONUT FLOUR

1/2 TEASPOON BAKING POWDER

1/4 TEASPOON BAKING SODA

1 TEASPOON GARLIC POWDER

5 TABLESPOONS PLANT-BASED BUTTER, MELTED

2 CUPS FRESH PLANT-BASED PARMESAN CHEESE, GRATED

1   Preheat the oven to 400 degrees and line a baking sheet with parchment paper.

2   Combine the dry ingredients in a large bowl. Pour in the melted butter and cheese. Stir the dough well; the batter will be very stiff.

3   Using a melon scoop, arrange the dough on the baking sheet. Use a fork dipped in water to press the cheese straw flat.

4   Bake for 8-10 minutes.

5   Cool completely and store in an airtight container.

# SAVORY OLIVE AND ROSEMARY BREAD PUDDING

*I created this recipe for my husband, Chris. He loves olives dearly, so I decided to combine them into a delicious savory bread pudding. This makes a wonderful side dish.*

1 CUP DICED SWEET ONION

2 TABLESPOONS CHOPPED FRESH ROSEMARY

1 TABLESPOON OLIVE OIL

1 LOAF GLUTEN-FREE BREAD

6 LARGE EGGS

2 CUPS PLAIN ALMOND MILK, UNSWEETENED

1 TEASPOON SALT

1/2 TEASPOON BLACK PEPPER

1/2 CUP SUN-DRIED TOMATOES IN OIL, DRAINED AND CHOPPED

1 CUP BLACK OLIVES, SLICED AND DRAINED

8 OUNCES PLANT-BASED CREAM CHEESE

1   Preheat the oven to 350 degrees and spray an oval casserole dish with non-stick cooking spray.

2   In a small skillet, sauté the onion and rosemary in the olive oil until the onions are soft, about 5 minutes. Remove the skillet from the heat.

3   Cut the bread into cubes and place it in a large bowl.

4   Whisk together the eggs, milk, salt, and pepper.

5   Pour the egg mixture over the bread. Stir in the onion and rosemary mixture, the sun-dried tomatoes, and the olives.

6   Pour the bread mixture into the casserole dish. Crumble the cream cheese over the top of the mixture.

7   Bake for 35-40 minutes.

# CHICKEN AND PORTOBELLO MUSHROOM POT PIE

*When it comes to savory baking, I love to go for a comfort food that reminds me of my childhood. Forget peas and carrots and put a new spin on the classic with this recipe.*

## FOR THE FILLING

1 CUP SWEET ONION, DICED

2 CUPS BABY PORTOBELLO MUSHROOMS, SLICED

2 TABLESPOONS OLIVE OIL

2 CUPS BONELESS, SKINLESS CHICKEN BREAST, COOKED

8 OUNCES PLANT-BASED CREAM CHEESE

1 CUP CHICKEN BROTH

1 TEASPOON HERBS DE PROVENCE

1   Preheat the oven to 350 degrees and spray a large cast-iron skillet with non-stick cooking spray.

2   Cook the onion and mushrooms together in the olive oil over medium heat until they are tender.

3   Shred the chicken and set aside.

4   Stir in the cream cheese and broth with the onions and mushrooms until well blended. Stir in the chicken and herbs de Provence.

5   Remove from the heat and pour the chicken mixture into the bottom of the skillet.

## FOR THE TOPPING

1 CUP ALMOND FLOUR

1 TEASPOON BAKING POWDER

1/2 TEASPOON FINE SEA SALT

1/2 TEASPOON HERBS DE PROVENCE

1 EGG

2 TABLESPOONS OLIVE OIL

1/2 CUP PLAIN ALMOND MILK

1   In a medium bowl, mix all of the ingredients together with a whisk.

2   Pour the topping over the chicken mixture and bake for 30 minutes.

# PUMPKIN CORNBREAD

*What happens when a classic Southern cornbread is combined with the fall flavor of pumpkin? Deliciousness!*

1 CUP ALMOND FLOUR

1 1/2 CUPS GLUTEN-FREE CORNMEAL

1/2 CUP COCONUT SUGAR

1 TEASPOON BAKING SODA

1 TEASPOON BAKING POWDER

1/2 TEASPOON FINE SEA SALT

1 CUP VANILLA ALMOND MILK, UNSWEETENED

1/2 CUP PLANT-BASED BUTTER, MELTED

1 EGG

1 CUP PUMPKIN PUREE (NOT PIE FILLING)

1 TEASPOON VANILLA

1   Preheat the oven to 375 degrees and grease a 9x13 baking dish.

2   In a large mixing bowl, combine the dry ingredients making sure that all is well blended.

3   In a separate bowl, whisk the wet ingredients together.

4   Pour the wet ingredients into the dry ingredients and blend well.

5   Pour the mixture into the baking dish and bake for 30 minutes, or until set.

# MAMA'S THANKSGIVING DRESSING

*I am one of those that can eat dressing year-round. I absolutely love it! My twist on my mama's dressing lets me continue to enjoy the flavors of my youth.*

2 CUPS ALMOND FLOUR

1 CUP CORNMEAL

2 TEASPOONS BAKING POWDER

2 TEASPOONS FINE SEA SALT

2 EGGS

1/3 CUP OLIVE OIL

1 CUP MILK

1 CUP CHOPPED RED BELL PEPPER

1 CUP CHOPPED GREEN BELL PEPPER

1 CUP CHOPPED CELERY

1 1/2 CUPS CHOPPED SWEET ONION

4 TABLESPOONS PLANT-BASED BUTTER, MELTED

3 EXTRA-LARGE EGGS, LIGHTLY BEATEN

1 1/2 CUPS CHICKEN BROTH OR HOMEMADE STOCK

1 TEASPOON COARSE BLACK PEPPER

1   Preheat the oven to 400 degrees and grease a 9x13 baking pan.

2   In a large mixing bowl, mix together the almond flour, cornmeal, baking powder, salt, eggs, olive oil, and milk.

3   Stir in the red and green peppers, celery, and onions.

4   In a small bowl, whisk together the butter, beaten eggs, broth, and pepper.

5   Pour the egg mixture into the flour mixture; stir well.

6   Pour into the baking pan and bake, uncovered, for 45–55 minutes.

HELPFUL TIP! When testing for doneness, be sure to test in the center of the dish, because some ovens cook faster than others.

# SPINACH AND FETA MUFFINS

*Don't let the simple ingredients in this muffin fool you; it is no wallflower! I love a bread with personality and this one is overflowing with it.*

2 CUPS ALMOND FLOUR

2 TEASPOONS BAKING POWDER

1 TEASPOON FINE SEA SALT

1 TEASPOON GARLIC POWDER

2 EGGS

1/3 CUP OLIVE OIL

9 OUNCES FROZEN SPINACH, THAWED AND DRAINED

1 CUP PLANT-BASED FETA CHEESE

1 CUP MILK

1   Preheat the oven to 350 degrees and line twelve muffin cups with paper liners.

2   Mix the dry ingredients together in a bowl.

3   Combine the wet ingredients in a separate bowl and mix well.

4   Add the dry ingredients to the wet ingredients.

5   Divide the mixture among the muffin cups and bake for 20 minutes.

# MIMI'S CHEESE STRAWS

*My Mimi always made cheese straws during the holidays. Cheese straws are perfect for parties, as well. I will often top them with a dollop of homemade strawberry preserves for parties and showers!*

1 1/4 CUPS ALMOND FLOUR, PACKED TIGHT

1/2 TEASPOON BAKING POWDER

1/4 TEASPOON BAKING SODA

1 TEASPOON CAYENNE PEPPER

5 TABLESPOONS PLANT-BASED BUTTER, MELTED

2 CUPS PLANT-BASED CHEDDAR CHEESE, SHREDDED AND AT ROOM TEMPERATURE

1   Preheat the oven to 400 degrees and line a baking sheet with parchment paper.

2   In a large bowl, combine the dry ingredients. Pour in the melted butter and cheese. Stir the dough well; the batter will be very stiff.

3   Using your hands, shape a melon ball-size scoop into a flat circle. Arrange the cheese straws on the baking sheet.

4   Bake for 8-10 minutes.

5   Cool completely and store in an airtight container.

# GARLIC AND HERB FLATBREAD

*When it is family movie night, this is always on the menu! I serve it with a little marinara for dipping!*

1 CUP PLANT-BASED MOZZARELLA

1/4 CUP ALMOND FLOUR

1 EGG, BEATEN

1/2 TEASPOON GARLIC POWDER

1/2 TEASPOON DRIED BASIL

1/2 TEASPOON DRIED OREGANO

1   Preheat the oven to 450 degrees.

2   Combine all ingredients in a large bowl.

3   Turn dough out onto parchment paper and press out evenly to 1/4-inch thickness.

4   Bake for 12 minutes.

# HERB BISCUITS

*Inspired by my love of a biscuit that I had in a tea room while traveling. Herbs de Provence is an aromatic herb that will transport you to southeast France.*

2 CUPS ALMOND FLOUR

2 TEASPOONS BAKING POWDER

1 TEASPOON FINE SEA SALT

1 TEASPOON HERBS DE PROVENCE

2 EGGS

1/3 CUP OLIVE OIL

1 CUP ALMOND MILK, UNSWEETENED

1    Preheat the oven to 350 degrees and line twelve muffin cups with paper liners.

2    Mix the dry ingredients together in a bowl.

3    Combine the wet ingredients in a separate bowl and mix well.

4    Add the dry ingredients to the wet ingredients.

5    Divide the mixture among the muffin cups and bake for 20-22 minutes.

# ALMOND FLOUR BISCUITS

*There isn't a Southern table that doesn't have a biscuit on it for family gatherings. These biscuits are perfect for breakfast, lunch, and dinner, and are delicious served with my fig butter or preserves.*

1/4 CUP PLANT-BASED GREEK YOGURT

1 EGG, BEATEN

1 CUP ALMOND FLOUR

2 TEASPOONS BAKING POWDER

1/2 TEASPOON FINE SEA SALT

1 TABLESPOON PLANT-BASED BUTTER, MELTED (OPTIONAL)

1   Preheat the oven to 350 degrees and line a baking sheet with parchment paper.

2   In a large bowl, whisk together the yogurt and the egg.

3   Stir in the almond flour, baking powder, and salt.

4   Evenly divide the batter into six biscuits and place onto the prepared baking sheet.

5   Bake the biscuits for 15–17 minutes. Remove from the oven and baste with melted butter (if desired) before serving.

CHAPTER 7

—

THIS AND
THAT

# FIG BUTTER

*Many of us grew up with apple butter on the table at breakfast. My twist with figs brings back summer memories of all of Daddy's fig trees.*

6 CUPS FRESH FIGS, WASHED AND STEMS
   REMOVED

3/4 CUP HONEY*

1/4 CUP FRESH LEMON JUICE

1/4 CUP WATER

2 TEASPOONS VANILLA

1 TEASPOON CINNAMON

1/2 TEASPOON NUTMEG

1/2 TEASPOON CLOVE

1    Add all the ingredients into a slow cooker and cook on low for 8 hours.

2    Allow the mixture to cool for a few minutes before carefully ladling the mixture into the blender to puree.

3    Pour the fig butter into hot canning jars and seal.

*For a richer flavor, I like to use date syrup instead of honey.

# FRUIT PRESERVES

Summer fruit preserves are something I grew up with. The ingredient amounts for these recipes change based on the fruit, but the directions are the same for all three, which makes it super easy to make homemade preserves to enjoy all year! I prefer honey in some and maple syrup in others, but you can go with your favorite! I use a potato masher to crush the fruit.

## STRAWBERRY PRESERVES

2 1/4 CUPS FRESH STRAWBERRIES, WASHED, STEMS REMOVED, AND CRUSHED

3 TABLESPOONS PECTIN

1 1/4 CUPS HONEY

## PEACH PRESERVES

2 CUPS FRESH PEACHES, WASHED, PEELED, CUT UP IN A BOWL, AND CRUSHED

3 TABLESPOONS PECTIN

2 TABLESPOONS FRESH LEMON JUICE

2/3 CUP PURE MAPLE SYRUP

## BLUEBERRY PRESERVES

4 CUPS FRESH BLUEBERRIES, WASHED AND CRUSHED

2 TABLESPOONS LEMON JUICE

6 TABLESPOONS PECTIN

1 1/2 CUPS PURE MAPLE SYRUP

1   For whichever preserves recipe you'd like, add everything except the sweetener to a large pot. Stirring constantly, bring the fruit to a boil over medium-high heat. This needs to be a boil that you cannot stir down!

2   Add your sweetener to the mixture and return it to the boiling point. While stirring constantly, boil the mixture for 1 full minute. Remove the pot from the heat and allow the mixture to cool slightly.

3   Spoon the preserves into prepared canning jars and seal.

# CHRISTOPHER'S PEPPER JELLY

My oldest son absolutely loves pepper jelly! Not only is it delicious on top of Parmesan cheese straws, but also on a million other things as well. Try it as a glaze for meats, adding it to barbecue sauce, or as a knock-out sandwich spread!

1 CUP CHOPPED JALAPEÑO PEPPERS, SEEDS REMOVED

1 CUP GREEN BELL PEPPERS, SEEDS REMOVED

1 1/2 CUPS WHITE VINEGAR

6 1/2 CUPS COCONUT SUGAR

JUICE OF ONE LEMON

6 TABLESPOONS PECTIN

1   Add the jalapeño peppers, green bell peppers, and white vinegar to a blender or food processor; blend until smooth.

2   Pour the mixture into a pot and add the coconut sugar and lemon juice. Bring the mixture to a boil, stirring several times while it comes to a boil. Boil the mixture for 1 minute and then remove from the heat.

3   Allow the mixture to sit for 5 minutes then stir in the pectin.

4   Divide the jelly among prepared canning jars and seal.

HELPFUL TIP! Always wear gloves when handling hot peppers (such as jalapeños) to avoid the burning sensation caused by capsaicin.

# WHIPPED CREAM

*The most classic topping for any dessert!*

~~~~~~~~~~~~~~~~~~~~~~~~~~~~~~~~~~~~~~~~~~~~~~~~~~~~~~~~~~~~~

8 OUNCES PLANT-BASED WHIPPING CREAM          4 TABLESPOONS POWDERED COCONUT SUGAR

1   Using a mixer on high, whip the cream in a mixing bowl until you see it begin to thicken. As you
    continue, add the coconut sugar one tablespoon at a time and continue whipping until stiff peaks form.

# POWDERED COCONUT SUGAR

*Powdered sugar is needed for many desserts, and now you can make your own!*

~~~~~~~~~~~~~~~~~~~~~~~~~~~~~~~~~~~~~~~~~~~~~~~~~~~~~~~~~~~~~

4 CUPS COCONUT SUGAR          4 TABLESPOONS TAPIOCA FLOUR

1   Place all ingredients in a blender and blend for 30-60 seconds. You will notice the powder beginning
    to stick to the sides of the blender. Wait 1 minute before removing the lid to allow the powder to settle.
    Store in an airtight container.

# LEMON CURD

Top gingerbread, use in a pie, top ice cream, or eat it straight from the jar! Lemon curd is one of my favorite things to take a dessert over the top. You can even stir some into whipped plant-based creams and use it as a fruit dip!

5 EGG YOLKS

1 CUP COCONUT SUGAR

1/3 CUP FRESH LEMON JUICE

ZEST OF 4 LEMONS

1/2 CUP PLANT-BASED BUTTER, CUT INTO CUBES

1    In a double boiler or a glass bowl over a saucepan, heat 1 inch of water to boiling. Whisk in the egg yolks and coconut sugar, then slowly pour in the lemon juice. Whisk the mixture constantly for about 7 minutes or until it begins to thicken.

2    Remove the mixture from the heat and add the butter, continuing to whisk until it has melted into the lemon mixture.

3    Pour the mixture into a glass bowl and cover it with plastic wrap. Push the plastic wrap all the way down to the curd to prevent a skin from forming.

4    Chill in the refrigerator for 2 hours. This will keep 10 days in the refrigerator or freeze for up to 3 months.

# CHOCOLATE SAUCE

*Drizzle this sauce on brownies, ice cream, a slice of pound cake, or even whip into cream—enjoy any way you can think! Chocolate always makes it better.*

8 OUNCES PLANT-BASED WHIPPING CREAM

1 CUP PURE MAPLE SYRUP

2 TABLESPOONS COCONUT SUGAR

3/4 CUP COCOA POWDER

1 TEASPOON VANILLA

1    In a saucepan over medium heat, combine the whipping cream, maple syrup, coconut sugar, and cocoa powder until smooth. Remove the mixture from the heat and stir in the vanilla. Store in the refrigerator.

# ABOUT THE AUTHOR

Lara Lyn Carter is an Emmy Award–winning television host, chef, and cookbook author and a two-time Taste Award winner. Her first cookbook, *Skinny Southern*, which is all gluten- and refined sugar-free cooking, climbed all the way to #2 on Amazon's Hot New Release list and sold out in 12 days. *Thyme for Sharing with Lara Lyn Carter*, which she hosted, created, and produced, aired the summer of 2015 as part of Georgia Public Broadcasting's summer cooking line-up and received excellent ratings and praise. The show was nominated for four Emmys in the categories of lighting, photography, director, and on-camera talent, for which Carter received her Emmy as host. In addition, Lara Lyn created and hosted *Savor the Good Life* with Raycom Media's WALB, the NBC and ABC affiliate in Southwest Georgia, for three years.

Lara Lyn is considered Georgia's "go to authority" on Southern entertaining. She converted to healthy, clean cooking and shares her vast experience and array of Southern recipes with a twist to her constantly growing followers. She has been featured on numerous television shows including The Food Network, as well as in magazines, newspapers, podcasts, and radio shows across the US and Canada.

Lara Lyn has entertained and cooked for people from coast to coast at numerous food and wine festivals including the Telluride Wine and Food Festival in Colorado and the Food Network South Beach Wine and Food Festival in Miami. Lara Lyn completed a major media tour in Canada in January 2017 for national media including television, radio, and filming live with Diply and Yahoo. She showed the Canadians her true Southern hospitality.

When not working, Lara Lyn keeps herself busy with her husband and their three sons, ages 22, 17, and 5. To learn more about Chef Lara Lyn Carter, please visit http://laralyncarter.com/

# ABOUT FAMILIUS

Familius is a book publisher dedicated to helping families be happy. We believe that the family is the fundamental unit of society and that happy families are the foundation of a happy life. The greatest work anyone will ever do will be within the walls of his or her own home. And we don't mean vacuuming! We recognize that every family looks different and passionately believe in helping all families find greater joy, whatever their situation. To that end, we publish beautiful books that help families live our 9 Habits of Happy Family Life:

- Love Together
- Play Together
- Learn Together
- Work Together
- Talk Together
- Heal Together
- Read Together
- Eat Together
- Laugh Together

Website: www.familius.com
Facebook: www.facebook.com/paterfamilius
Twitter: @familiustalk, @paterfamilius1
Pinterest: www.pinterest.com/familius

The most important work you ever do will be within the walls of your own home.

# CONVERSIONS

## VOLUME MEASUREMENTS

| U.S. | METRIC |
|------|--------|
| 1 teaspoon | 5 ml |
| 1 tablespoon | 15 ml |
| 1/4 cup | 60 ml |
| 1/3 cup | 75 ml |
| 1/2 cup | 125 ml |
| 2/3 cup | 150 ml |
| 3/4 cup | 175 ml |
| 1 cup | 250 ml |

## WEIGHT MEASUREMENTS

| U.S. | METRIC |
|------|--------|
| 1/2 ounce | 15 g |
| 1 ounce | 30 g |
| 3 ounces | 90g |
| 4 ounces | 115 g |
| 8 ounces | 225 g |
| 12 ounces | 350 g |
| 1 pound | 450 g |
| 2 1/4 pounds | 1 kg |

## TEMPERATURE CONVERSION

| FAHRENHEIT | CELSIUS |
|------------|---------|
| 250 | 120 |
| 300 | 150 |
| 325 | 160 |
| 350 | 180 |
| 375 | 190 |
| 400 | 200 |
| 425 | 220 |
| 450 | 230 |